Angels on Assignment

SEUN IJIYOKUN

Elovis Publishing Group

"There is a story in everyone~"

on Assignment

ight © 2015 by Seun Ijiyokun

lished by:

eviv Publishing Group
Houston, TX 77082
www.elevivpublishinggroup.com
1-713-730-5071

ISBN-13: 978-0692458273
ISBN-10: 0692458271

Scripture quotations are taken from the King James Version.
Public Domain

Printed in the United States of America

Dedication

This book is dedicated to my children Joseph, David, and Grace

To my lovely wife Tosin Ijiyokun.

To all the men of God, friends, and families who have being a tremendous blessing to me in the journey of life: you are Godly angels and divine counselors to the path of truth.
"Where there is no counsel the people fall; But in the multitude of counselors there is safety." Proverb 11:14.

Lastly to my Mother, Deaconess Racheal Omoyeni Ijiyokun, you are blessed.

Foreword

The importance of the ministry of Angels in the life of the Believer cannot be underestimated; even Christ, himself, was ministered to by Angels. If the Son of God needed the ministry of Angels, how much more do today's Believers? Whether you have recognized it or not, Angels are very active executing assignments for God. It is high time for every present-day Believer to develop an awareness of this ministry, and allow himself to fully experience it. This book seeks to illuminate the Angelic ministry in the life of the Believer, so that he will begin to recognize, understand, and maximize it. Read it prayerfully and take advantage of this great ministry that God has for His children. It is insightful and will remind you that you are not alone. *"For he shall give his Angels charge over thee, to keep thee in all thy ways."* Psalm 91:11.

Apostle Matthew Oluwajoba
General Overseer Christ United Ministry International

Introduction

"And he was there in the wilderness forty days, tempted of Satan; and was with the wild beasts; and the Angels ministered unto him." Mark 1:13

This was an agonizing experience for Jesus in the wilderness--but He permitted the lesser (the Angels) to minister to him-the greater one (Savior). Being created in the image of God, you, too, need the assistance of Angels. Their importance will be apparent as they will come at different times in your life to minister to you, both spiritually and physically. *Are they not all ministering spirits, sent forth to minister for them who shall be heirs of salvation?* Heb. 1:14

As Angels are not readily visible, we need God's grace to discern those who are dispatched from Heaven to assist us, lest we run the risk of haphazardly becoming an obstacle to the Angel's mission. Through the course of this book, I will address Angels figuratively as both physical and spiritual beings, in order to effectively convey some insights regarding the Angelic ministry.

Angels are benevolent to mankind from cradle to grave: whenever a child is born, there is an intercession of Angels who, I refer to as *"helpers of destiny."* These are the people who help facilitate the birth. At death, certain people are also responsible for the burial. The life of Moses demonstrates this premise as his "birth" into his destiny was facilitated by Angelic intervention, with the papyrus basket being kept afloat and unnoticed until just the right time in Exodus 2:3.

When he died, the Bible says that God buried him, which I believe was with the help of Angels Exodus 33:5-6. The ministry of the Angels continues even after death; they are responsible for escorting our spiritual bodies to Abraham's bosom. Luke 16:22 says *"And it came to pass, that the beggar died, and was carried by the Angels into Abraham's bosom: the rich man also died, and was buried,"*

After his death, the spiritual body of Moses was conveyed to heaven by Michael, the Archangel in Jude 1:9. This signifies that Angels play a vital role throughout our entire lifespan on earth —and beyond.

Our citizenship is in heaven, from which we also eagerly wait for the savior, the Lord Jesus Christ, who will transform our lowly body that it may be conformed to His glorious body, according to the working by which He is able even to subdue all things to Himself, Philippians 3:20-21.

No one can see God with a corruptible body all must be transformed before approaching the throne of grace. For the eyes of God are too pure than to behold an iniquity. Habakkuk 1:13 says, *"Thou art of purer eyes than to behold evil, and canst not look on iniquity: wherefore lookest thou upon them that deal treacherously, and holdest thy tongue when the wicked devoureth the man that is more righteous than he?"* The Angels will be assigned to transform our lowly body.

Angels are spiritually empowered by God to carry out specific assignments for man. The recognition of the purpose of Angels is not limited to the Old Testament scriptures; the impact of Angels is quite enormous in the New Testament! Angels were a major part of life in the early church, and are mentioned more than 180 times in the New Testament, alone. By my finite knowledge of an apostolic ministry, Angels are very good instrument in the hand of the Lord. They do not have powers of their own; they are commissioned and ordained by God-- just as a shepherd (pastor) is ordained or commissioned for a church and are responsible for its care both day and night. *"And I will give you pastors according to mine heart, which shall feed you with knowledge and understanding"* Jeremiah 3:15. In the same manner, Angels are to guide and protect man; they are servants to man. *"For He shall give His Angels charge over you in all your ways; they shall bear thee up in their hands, lest thou dash thy foot against a stone."* (Psalm 91:11-12).

Angels are monitoring spirits for man. God's love toward man is so enormous that He has commissioned Angels to watch over them day and night. Psalm 121:3-4 says, *"He will not suffer thy foot to be moved: he that keepeth thee will not slumber. Behold, he that keepeth Israel shall neither slumber nor sleep"* Also Heb. 2:6-7, *"But one in a certain place testified, saying, What is man, that thou art mindful of him? or the son of man, that thou visitest him? Thou madest him a little lower than the Angels; thou crownedst him with glory and honour, and didst set him over the works of thy hands:"* see Psalm 8:3-5.

Angels are not so superior to man, but their importance to man cannot be under-estimated-- both in heaven and on earth. According to the scripture in 1 Corinthians 13:9; *"For we know in part and we prophecy in part",* so my perspective of Angels is not absolute but only a partial revelation of what they may portray-- there could very well be other aspects of their ministry not yet made known to me; as no one can see or say it all.

"And I beheld, and I heard the voice of many Angels round about the throne and the beasts and the elders: and the number of them was ten thousand times ten thousand, and thousands of thousands; Saying with a loud voice, Worthy is the Lamb that was slain to receive power, and

riches, and wisdom, and strength, and honour, and glory, and blessing" Rev 5:11-12.

Angels reside in Heaven, but they are often sent to earth by God to carry out some supernatural assignments that are beyond the strength of man. Angels are not to be worshiped; they are our fellow servants. They have no power of their own, they can never take the glory of God in man's life neither can they occupy the position of God. *And I John saw these things, and heard them. And when I had heard and seen, I fell down to worship before the feet of the Angel which shewed me these things. Then saith he unto me, See thou do it not: for I am thy fellow servant, and of thy brethren the prophets, and of them which keep the sayings of this book: worship God. (*Rev 22:8-9).

Angels are working for the Trinity; they represent God the Father, the Son and the Holy Spirit. The presence of God is often indicated by the appearance of Angels; they are messengers-- vessels through which the promise or the counsel of God is brought to man.   *"That confirmeth the word of His servant, and performeth the counsel of His messengers; that saith to Jerusalem, Thou shalt be inhabited; and to the cities of Judah, Ye shall be built, and I will raise up the decayed places thereof:"* (Isaiah 44:26). Angels are messengers of God. When Mary asked the Angel how can this be, since I do not know a man? *"And the Angel answered and said unto her, The Holy Ghost shall come upon thee, and the power of the Highest shall overshadow thee: therefore also that holy thing which shall be born of thee shall be called the Son of God."* Luke1:34-35. This is to unravel that the Angels are witnessing for the Trinity anytime they are on assignment.

When God sent his Angel to a man, whatever the Angel instructed or commanded and said was the replica of God's voice. Psalm 62:11 says *"God hath spoken once; twice have I heard this; that power belongeth unto God."* Whatever the Angel said will be confirmed by God. They do not have power but God who spoke through them ensure the word does not fall to the ground. Ecclesiastes 8:4 says, *"Where the word of a king is, there is power: and who may say unto him, What doest thou?"* Whenever God spoke through His Angel, His servants or a fellow brothers and sisters they are to accomplish a purpose. According to Amos 3:7, *"Surely the Lord GOD will do nothing, but he revealeth his secret unto His servants the prophets".* Your Angel may not necessarily come in white garment with wings as we often imagine, but as a human fellow who has been empowered to reveal the mind of God concerning your situation.

For as the rain cometh down, and the snow from heaven, and returneth not thither, but watereth the earth, and maketh it bring forth and bud, that it may give seed to the sower, and bread to the eater: So shall my word be that goeth forth out of my mouth: it shall not return unto me void, but it shall accomplish that which I please, and it shall prosper in the thing whereto I sent it. Isaiah 55:10-11. God uses a vessel to convey His word or promises and that vessel is the Angel. Hallelujah!

I pray that the anointing of the Holy Spirit will be on this book in a powerful way to bring revelation and freedom to you as a vessel of honor unto God and His Kingdom. Amen!

TABLE OF CONTENTS

Angels have no philosophy but "LOVE"
~ **Terry Guillemet**

CHAPTER 1

NATURE OF ANGELS AND THEIR MODUS OPERANDI

For a better understanding of Angels it is good to exploit their nature or characteristic and how God has made them accessible to man. *Who maketh his Angels spirits; his ministers a flaming fire:* – Psalm 104:4 & Hebrew1:7. Going by the above scriptures, generally Angels are spirit, not often visible to the naked eye but through wisdom, God's Angels can manifest in two forms in order to carry out their   assignments.

(i) **Angels in the spirit**
(ii) **Angels in the appearance of man**

Angels in the Spirit (Humanoid or Supernatural being)

Angels can manifest in their divine natural being not in human attire but in a heavenly designed pure white garment with wings, Matthew 28:3, Daniel 10:4-7. Like ghosts not visible to a naked eye but can be seen by sacred eye. They are mostly seen by anointed men of God who God has given the grace to see beyond the physical world and have access to the realm of the spirit (prophet) or a seer 1 Samuel 9:9.

2 King 6:15-17: *"And when the servant of the man of God was risen early, and gone forth, behold, an host compassed the city both with horses and chariots. And his servant said unto him, Alas, my master! how shall we do? And he answered, Fear not: for they that be with us are more than they that be with them. And Elisha prayed, and said, LORD, I pray thee, open his eyes, that he may see. And the LORD opened the eyes of the young man; and he saw: and, behold, the mountain was full of horses and chariots of fire round about Elisha."* (Angelic host of heaven).

Hebrew 12:21-22: *"And so terrible was the sight, that Moses said, I exceedingly fear and quake:) But ye are come unto mount Sion, and unto the city of the living God, the heavenly Jerusalem, and to an innumerable company of Angels,"*

Great and anointed men of God have the ability to see Angels. It is a level or status in the spirit. These Angels descend from heaven during ministration, be it at a church service, crusades and any Christian gathering; their mission is to perform all kind of miracles. They bring all kinds of blessings to men. They are heavenly couriers. That is why many Christian gatherings are not for fun, they are always taken over by ministering Angels. God uses them to cause deliverance from bondage and yoke.

"And the whole multitude of the people were praying without at the time of incense. And there appeared unto him an Angel of the Lord standing on the right side of the

altar of incense. And when Zacharias saw him, he was troubled, and fear fell upon him. "Luke 1:10-12

Angels in the appearance of man (Natural being)

This is the most common way Angels can manifest to carry out their heavenly assignment because God made them spirits; they can come down and assume the position of man [Adamic nature] so that they appear friendly, as opposed to being revealed in their divine nature, appearing intimidating-- this makes them accessible to man. They can communicate, eat, or drink-- this was the experience of Abraham in Gen 18:1-10. Most of the time, we need grace to see or discern when Angels come across our way so that we can receive what they brought. Out of ignorance many have abused, rejected or even cursed their Angel that would be addressed in-depth in other chapters.

Angels are at times someone you consider to be a stranger, or someone who isn't cordial with you. There was an incident narrated by a man of God in Nigeria, Pastor Ayo Oritsejafor in one of his meetings. He spoke about a Christian sister in his church whose promotion was denied for several years at work. One day at the board meeting, the boss who is an atheist, stood up to ask why the Christian sister hasn't been promoted all these years, the board members were in shock to hear him plead for her promotion but promised to look into it.

At the close of another meeting he raises the same question, the board can no longer defer the issue of that sister, they passed a resolution and she was promoted right away. After the promotion, one of the attendees in the meeting had to confide in the lady on how her promotion on the job was initiated and expedited by the atheist boss. She was surprised and proceeded to thank her atheist boss but surprisingly the boss dragged her out of his office saying, *"I don't know what you are talking about".*

The sister ran out with tears and went to the man of God narrating her ordeal. The man of God said to her, you need to thank God; he has only acted as your Angel to fight for your right without him knowing what he was doing. He has completed the Angelic assignment on your behalf, therefore stay away from him. I pray that the Angel of the Lord will intercede on your behalf over all your delayed blessings.

The point or wisdom in this testimony is that God can use anybody for you as an Angel in disguise; either a strange fellow or familiar person to you. The doors Angels do not open remain closed. Therefore as a believer we should learn to pray that God should send His Angel in form of man to bring His help across our way. Proverb 21:1 says ***"The king's heart is in the hand of the LORD, as the rivers of water: he turneth it whithersoever he will."*** So God can turn anybody's heart to favor or help you in difficult situations of life. It can be your boss, your subordinate, anybody you can ever imagine so far the person has a heart that works, and that God can turn to favor you. Specifically in Luke 2:52 and 1 Samuel 2:26 the bible tells of Jesus Christ and Samuel that they enjoy the favor of God and of men in life. I have personally experienced the help of Angels in the appearance of man who helped me in the past having prayed day and night for God to change my story. This I would narrate in the next few pages of this book.

I would like you to pray this powerful prayer:

1. Oh Lord, let your Angel descend in the likeness of man and lead me through the journey of life in the mighty name of Jesus. (Act 12:7-11)

2. Oh Lord, let me experience the help of Angels in the area of my

finances, marriage, ministry, and career this year in the mighty name of Jesus.

3. Father let your innumerable hosts of heaven (Angels) fight my

battles this year in the mighty name of Jesus.

"For mine Angel shall go before thee, and bring thee in unto the Amorites, and the Hittites, and the Perizzites, and the Canaanites, and the Hivites, and the Jebusites: and I will cut them off." Exodus 23:23

These three prayers are simple but powerful than a ballistic missile or any atomic bomb if only you can pray it with courage and understanding of the revelation that Angels are on assignment for you.

The wings of angel are often found on the back of the least likely people.
~ Eric Honeycutt.

CHAPTER 2

ANGELS ARE DIVINE HELPERS OF DESTINY

On many occasions I wonder why a man should suffer perpetually when there are innumerable host of Angels in heaven, and only one is enough to make a change in one's life; if only God can release them to work. Overtime I have learned that prayer is the force that triggers God to send them to work whenever there is a need.

Mathew 26:52-53 says: *"Then said Jesus unto him, Put up again thy sword into his place: for all they that take the sword shall perish with the sword. Thinkest thou that I cannot now pray to my Father, and he shall presently give me more than twelve legions of angels?"*

I don't know the kind of Angels you want or where exactly you want them to work for you, but by virtue of that verse I think prayer can help. The bible spoke about the prophet Daniel who prayed for a specific blessing and God responded by sending one Angel to him but when he noticed a delay, he persisted and God sent another (no nonsense) or a radical Angel to get the blessing across the second heavens where the demons parades and operates, for the blessing to come down to Daniel (Daniel 10:12-13). Delay is not denial if only you do not relent in your prayers; if anybody has taken it upon himself to withhold your blessings may the Angels of the Lord intervene on your behalf and get your blessings across to you in Jesus name Amen.

There are Angels who show up as helpers of destiny, this was a typical example of David's experience in the book of 1 Chronicle 12:1-40. In this chapter, the Lord sent Angels in form of helpers of destiny to David while his life was in jeopardy. A critical analysis of this chapter reveals the seven qualities of these Angels whom God uses to help David.

1. **They are mighty men of valor (great people) man of influence.**
2. **Helpers in war (fire fighters)**
3. **Trained and experience people (experts)**
4. **Their faces are like lion faces (Frightening, radical, undiscouraged, and determined helpers)**
5. **Able to use left and right hands (being able to exhaust every avenue making use of every available resources to achieve their mission to help)**
6. **Equipped with different kinds of weapons. They were as swift as gazette on mountains (they are extraordinary people empowered by God to bring restoration).**
7. **People with understanding of time and season (men of Issachar). They are great counselors, prophets, teachers, good listeners, and encouragers in times of battles of life. They are vision promoters. Because the Holy Spirit has moved them to assist you they**

will discharge the entire ministry of the Holy Spirit
according to John 16:7, the amplified version:
 (1) COUNSELOR
 (2) HELPER
 (3)ADVOCATES
 (4) INTERCESSOR
 (5) STRENGTHENER
 (6) STANDBY
If God has sent across your way an Angel in form of man he
 or she
will be willing to carry out the above duties without been
 forced.

Verse 38 of the chapter concluded that all these men **were
people with loyal heart,** a good observation of verse 18 of this
chapter shows that God has dispatched the troops to help
David. David did not order for them, but on their own accord
they manifested from nowhere.

Brethren I don't know what you are experiencing right now,
you need the help of these godly assigned Angels. All the
aforementioned qualities of those helpers of destiny are very
important. A single person can possess these kinds of attributes
if truly God has sent them to you. So also God can send a group
of people, a church, family members, government, organization,
a society or community to stand in this same gap for you if only
you can understand this simple revelation of the Angels on
assignment and key into it to ask God for your own divine
intervention through the help of Angels.

In the gospel of Saint Mark 2:3, it was reported that four
men determined to bring the paralytic man to Christ for healing,
incidentally the same story was narrated by Luke who did not
acknowledge the importance of number because he was a

physician (Colossians 4:14) He sees just the healing experience of the paralytic man as narrated in the book of Luke 5:18-19. But Mark give the same account making reference to the **FOUR {4}** men which were Angels in disguise to help the paralytic man in spite of obstacles. There are people who can go the extra mile to help in life. I need them, you also need their help, and may the Lord send them to us in Jesus name. By divine revelation God can raise people from four distinct sources to help us in life.

(1) **Members of an extended or nuclear family**
(2) **Religious group like Churches etc.**
(3) **Friends from any directions**
(4) **The Governments, be it state or federal.**

I will expatiate on this in the later chapters. I am not too surprised that David got this kind of help as was narrated in 1 Chronicles 12 because he was a man of prayer, so Angels trooped down to move people in order to help him. In Psalm 86:17 He prayed that God should show him a sign for good that those who hate him may see it and be ashamed. Until God shows you a sign for good your enemy will keep laughing and mocking you; but the moment He releases His Angels to minister grace to you, your enemy is nothing but your footstool. (Psalm 110:1).

Another practical example was the event in Mathew 28:2-4: *"And, behold, there was a great earthquake: for the angel of the Lord descended from heaven, and came and rolled back the stone from the door, and sat upon it. His countenance was like lightning, and his raiment white as snow: And for fear of him the keepers did shake, and became as dead men."*

This sounds very interesting as God sent a radical Angel who looks dreadful to part the way for the Lord with nobody to stop him on his assignment. Jesus Christ was silent in the grave and the enemies, His accuser were laughing and mocking but at the break of dawn on the third day God releases His Angel and the enemy was disgraced. I pray that you will experience the same grace. Your Angel will deliver your blessings this year; your help will not be hindered in Jesus name.

If the Lord can enjoy the help of Angels for Him to resurrect and the enemy was disgraced, you and I are not left out, we need godly assigned Angels to take us far and to the place of destiny. It is quite pertinent to mention that the good news about the coming of the Lord Jesus was presented by the Angel; therefore I pray that God will send people on your way to give you the ideas, information, and good news for you to advance in your business, marriage, finance, career, and ministry this year. Amen

SEVEN THINGS GOD CAN USE THE ANGEL TO ACCOMPLISH FOR YOU

If God does something in the past He can still do it again, the essence of the miracles and events recorded in the scripture is to inform that God can still do exactly the same thing because *He is the same yesterday, today and forever. (*Hebrew 13:8) Therefore we shall exploit some principal roles played by the Angels of the Lord in the scripture and anchor our faith on God to experience the same miracle.

1. GOD CAN USE THEM TO PERFECT YOUR HEALING

In John 5:2-4: *"Now there is at Jerusalem by the sheep market a pool, which is called in the Hebrew tongue Bethesda, having five porches. In these lay a great multitude of impotent folk, of blind, halt, withered, waiting for the moving of the water. For an angel went down at a certain season into the pool, and troubled the water: whosoever then first after the troubling of the water stepped in was made whole of whatsoever disease he had."*

God can use His ministers to bring down the healing power of God. Psalm 104:4 says: *"He made them flame of fire, by virtue of their ministration they are stirring the waters for your healings."* All you need to do is key in your faith at this time and healing from heaven through the preaching of the word of God will make you whole. The scripture said, *"He sent his words and he heals them, and delivered them from their destruction."* Psalm 107:20.

2. HELP YOU TO SECURE A SPOUSE

The bible recorded in Gen 24:7, how Abraham trusted the Lord to send His Angel before His servant to secure a wife for Isaac. If you trust God for a wife or husband, you can ask God for directions through His Angel. I mean somebody who can lead you right and give you quality information about the spouse you are believing God for.

Mathew 1:19-20, Joseph would have called it quit with Virgin Mary and somebody else would have become her husband and Joseph would not have been acclaimed as the earthly father of Jesus Christ but God used an Angel to establish their relationship. This year is your year, you will get married by the help of God's Angel in Jesus name.

3. DELIVERANCE FROM BARRENNESS

On many occasions God has used His Angels to open the doors of fruitfulness to those who trust the Lord for the fruit of the womb. This was the experience of Abraham and Sarah Gen 18:13-14, Zechariah and Elizabeth in Luke 1:5-15, Manoah and his wife in Judges 13:6-7. God can send His prophets to you and give you a word concerning your fruitfulness in marriage and God will confirm his word. Amos 3:7 says, *"Surely the Lord God will do nothing, but he revealeth his secret unto his servants the prophets."* These are typical Angels that God can send to break the yokes of barrenness or delay in your marriage. It does not matter how long you've been waiting; this year will terminate your years of barrenness in Jesus name. Isaiah 40:31 *"But those who wait on the lord He shall renew their strength they shall mount up with wings like eagles, they shall run and not be weary they shall walk and not faint."*

4. TO DISARM YOUR HOUSEHOLD ENEMY

God can use his Angels to disarm your household enemy. Daniel 6:22 says, *"My God hath sent his angel, and hath shut the lions' mouths, that they have not hurt me: forasmuch as before him innocency was found in me; and also before thee, O king, have I done no hurt."* God used His Angel to save Daniel from the den of lions. He was a governor over a kingdom together with two other governors who were to control the affairs of the kingdom along with 120 Satraps of the kingdom but he was set up for destruction by those who are very

close and important to him. As you go this year the Lord will
assign his Angel to disarm your household enemies.

Apostle Paul said *"Notwithstanding the Lord stood with
me, and strengthened me; that by me the preaching might
be fully known, and that all the Gentiles might hear: and I
was delivered out of the mouth of the lion."* 2 Timothy 4:17.
Figuratively, lions are wicked enemies or evil people around our
vision, marriage, career, ministry, and finances. May the Angel
of the Lord strike them down as promised in Acts 12:23.

5. DELIVERANCE FROM SPIRITUAL AND PHYSICAL IMPRISONMENT IN LIFE

God can use His Angels to set you free from both physical
and spiritual imprisonment. Psalm 102:19-20 says, *for He
looked down from the height of his sanctuary, from heaven
the Lord viewed the earth to hear the groaning of the
prisoner, to release those appointed to death.* This was the
experience of Peter in Act 12:1-10, he was imprisoned and
appointed to death but the Lord raised an Angel to set him free.
If you are under any kind of demonic or satanic imprisonment,
the Angel of the Lord will lose you and show you the road to life
in Jesus name. Nahum 1:13 says, *for now I will break off his
yoke from you and burst your bonds asunder.* You are not
destined for imprisonment, I see God working on your behalf
this year as the Angel of the Lord will act as a jail breaker in your
interest and you will come out in Jesus name.

6. VISIONS AND REVELATIONS

God can use His Angels to give you visions and revelations about something important to you and others; be it your business, marriage, ministry, and career. Rev 1:1 says, *"The revelation of Jesus Christ which God gave him to show his servants things which must shortly take place. And He sent and signified it by His Angels to His servant John"*. Angels can show you things and tell you the interpretation; this was the experience of Zechariah in Zech 4:1-7. I pray that God will use His Angels, prophets, and Godly servants to show you mysteries of life; great and mighty things, hidden riches in Jesus name.

In Heaven an angel is nobody in particular

The difference between a successful man and a poor man is information; if you lack information you will lack progress. Not all stagnation is hereditary but due to lack of information; when someone is not informed he or she is automatically deformed.

~ George Bernard Shaw.

Many people are unemployed not because there is no job, no connection or viable information that will get them across to the place of destiny.   Hosea 4:6, *"my people perish for lack of knowledge"*, **vision and/or information.** The best source of information is **people.** We need an Angel to give us a clue on where, when and how to make it in life. Jeremiah 33:3 says *"Call to me and I will show you great and mighty things which you do not know"*.

7. ROLLING AWAY BARRIERS

Lastly, God can use His Angels to roll away barriers, Mark 16:3-5*, "and they said among themselves who will roll away* *the stone from the door of the tomb for us? But when they looked up they saw that the stone had been rolled away for it was very large. And entering the tomb they saw a young man clothed in a long white robe sitting on the right side (Angel) and they were alarmed"*. If God can do it for Jesus through an Angel, He can do it for you and I. This year I stand on the covenant of grace and I decree that every barrier to your riches, fruitfulness, healing, anointing, and power to be rolled away by the Lord's Angels in the mighty name of Jesus.

ANGEL IS A STRENGHTNER

Above all, God can send His Angel to strengthen you whenever you are weak and lose strength due to burdens in your heart. It doesn't matter how strong you think you are spiritually when you are weak and heavy laden, encumbered with a load of care you need somebody which can be your Angel at that time to keep you awake and help you move on. Many times I feel weak and troubled due to what I am passing through but when I receive the ministrations of the men of God I automatically regain my strength. According to Bill Withers in his *Lean on me Lyrics;*

'Sometimes in our lives we all have pain.
We all have sorrow,
 But if we are wise,
We know that there's always tomorrow.

Lean on me when you are not strong
And I'll be your friend,
I'll help you carry on
For it won't be long
Till I'm gonna need
Somebody to lean on.

Please swallow your pride
If I have things you need to borrow
For no one can fill those of your needs
That you don't let show

If there is a load you have to bear
That you can't carry
I am right up the road
I'll share your load
If you just call me

So just call me brother, when you need a hand
We all need somebody to lean on
I just might have a problem that you'd understand
We all need somebody to lean on.
Hallelujah!

We all need somebody from God to bring us words of faith and encouragement that would help get us back on track. That person might be a friend, wife, husband, pastor, church member, parent or guardian.

Luke 22:43-44, *"then the Angel appeared to him from heaven strengthening Him. And being in agony He prayed more earnestly. Then his sweat became like great drop of blood falling down to the ground."*

Brethren I don't know what you feel about the revelation of the Angels on assignment but I perceive in my spirit that God wants to put His Angels to work. I am not writing to promote the Angels beyond their level of duty but I say they are instruments in the hand of God to move mountains.

Habakkuk 3:6, *"He stood, and measured the earth: he beheld, and drove asunder the nations; and the everlast-*

*ing mountains were scattered, the perpetual hills did
bow: his ways are everlasting."*
Psalm 97:5 says, *"The hills melted like wax at the presence of the Lord, at the presence of the Lord of the
whole earth."*
Psalm 114:4 says, *"The mountain skipped like ram and
little hills like lamb".*
Zechariah 4:7, *"who are thou mountain before you and I,
they shall become plain this year in the mighty name of
Jesus."*
I Samuel 2:9 says, *"He will guard the fact of his saints,
but the wicked shall be silent in darkness, "For by
strength no man shall prevail".*

I don't know how long you have been struggling, and apply-
ing your strength to life's trials but I come to announce to you
through this little book that supernatural help is available
through Jesus Christ. *"For this purpose the son of God
manifest to destroy the work of the devil."* 1 John 3:8

ASK FOR ANGELIC ASSISTANCE IN
ALL YOUR UNDERTAKINGS

God can raise His Angels to conduct a naming ceremony,
marriage ceremony, any kind of operations in the hospital, court
jurisdiction, your interview in the embassy, interview for job
employment or contract award or any kind of promotion
assessment, your loan approval in the bank, your political and
electoral ambitions, your immigration status in the foreign land
and the hosts of other desires and aspirations that your strength
may not scale you through. If only you can access the throne
room of heaven to employ the assistance of Angels you shall

surely have a way out and your testimony will be great. *"He will keep the feet of his saints, and the wicked shall be silent in darkness; for by strength shall no man prevail."* 1 Samuel 2:9.

I had listened to a testimony of a servant of God who at the point of entry to a country at the embassy the Angel of the lord went ahead and changed his visiting visa to a permanent residence card. God is an omnipotent king, *"He is a God of all flesh nothing is too hard for Him"* Jeremiah 32:27.

DO NOT SEEK THE ASSISTANCE OF SATANIC ANGELS

Psalm 16:4 says, *"their sorrows shall be multiplied who hastens after another god."* Whatever God can offer, Satan has a counterfeit or what I call short-cut, but alas! victims of short cuts are often cut short. Don't employ satanic Angels to work for you. According to Revelations 12:7-9 when Satan or the serpent of old was cast down to the earth his Angels came down with him about one third of the Angels in heaven de-camped and joined Satan .

I am not daunted to disclose that the world is filled with false brethren. They are all over the place as they were assigned by the devil to cut the life of their victims short. But the scripture spoke concerning you and I in I Peter 2:9, *"But ye are a chosen generation, a royal priesthood, an holy nation, a peculiar people; that ye should shew forth the praises of him who hath called you out of darkness into his marvellous light;"*

Mathew 5:14. *"Ye are the light of the world. A city that is set on an hill cannot be hid."*

"Wherefore, my beloved, as ye have always obeyed, not as in my presence only, but now much more in my absence, work out your own salvation with fear and trembling." Philippians 2:12

The Lord has rated you and I, as the salt of the earth, therefore employing satanic Angels will cause the salt to be useless. Mathew 5:13 says, *"You are the salt of the earth but if the salt loses its flavor, how shall it be seasoned? It is then good for nothing but to be thrown out and trampled underfoot by men".* May we not be ensnared by the assistance of demonic Angels. I read a little about demonology, therefore I know there is a world of demons and they have hierarchy but the scripture says Jesus is the head of principality and powers in Colossians 2:10.

Revelation 9:11, *"and they had as king over them, the Angel of the bottomless pit, whose name in Hebrew is Abandon but in Greek he has name Apollyon".*

It was also revealed in Luke 11:15 that the Lord was erroneously accused of casting out demon by Beelzebub the ruler of the demons. It therefore means demons are in ranks, they also have rulers, and they are organized like any other religious settings. There are herbalists, sorcerers, witches and wizards, diverse occultist groups, death spirits, demons of the bottomless pit, principalities, and powers in the heavenlies, the oceanic or marine spirits. But they all confess that Jesus Christ is the Lord as seen in Mark 1:23-24. More so the bible recorded in Philippian 2:9 *"Therefore God has highly exalted Him and given him the name which is above every name, that at the name of Jesus every knee should bow of those in heaven and of those on earth and those under the earth, and that every tongue should confess that Jesus Christ is the Lord to the glory of God the father"*

Your delay is not a license to take a short cut but persistency with God will provide a lasting rest. Isaiah 62:7 says, *"Gives him no rest till He establishes and till He makes Jerusalem praise on earth".*

Pay attention to your dreams –
God's angels often speak directly to our hearts when we asleep.
~ Eileen Elias Freeman 1994

CHAPTER 3

RECALLING YOUR ANGELS TO WORK

Most people at one point in time enjoyed the assistance of godly assigned Angels but are now experiencing delays in certain areas of life. You can recall your Angels to come and work for you in whatever areas you desire. The same Angels that gave Peter freedom from prison came back to ensure that king Herod was beaten down. He returned to complete his assignment Acts 12:23 says, *"And immediately the angel of the Lord smote him, because he gave not God the glory: and he was eaten of worms, and gave up the ghost."* I don't know what Angels has started in your life, you need him to come back and complete his assignment. Zech 4:1, *"And the angel that talked with me came again, and waked me, as a man that is wakened out of his sleep."*

Judges 13:9 says, *"And God hearkened to the voice of Manoah; and the angel of God came again unto the woman as she sat in the field: but Manoah her husband was not with her."*

The power of life and death lies in your tongue, you can always ask God to send your Angels back to you to complete whatever he has started with you. Peradventure your Angel has retreated or quit because of your sinful or crooked lifestyle, you can always seek forgiveness and retrace your steps back to Gods kingdom, Psalm 30:5 say's *"For his anger endureth but a moment; in his favour is life: weeping may endure for a night, but joy cometh in the morning."* He will put your Angel back to work and whatever the Lord has started He will complete. *"Being confident of this very thing, that he which hath begun a good work in you will perform it until the day of Jesus Christ:"*- Amen   Philippians 1:6.

I would like to share my personal experience that God used an Angel in the appearance of man to deliver my blessings.

The wings of angel are often found on the back of the least likely people.

Eric Honeycutt

A few years ago I was working for a church in Lagos, Nigeria. As the account/admin officer for the church, I went out on a Monday morning to carry out some bank transactions for the church, on approaching the bank right in the Oyingbo market, a lady came to me and persuaded me to take advantage of the diversity visa lottery promotion. I told her, if that is why she had stopped me, then I wasn't interested. But the lady wouldn't let me go; she kept bugging and persuading me. In order to avoid embarrassment, I asked her how much, she said a single entry was 300 naira and for couples it was 500 naira; *"I don't have that kind of money now"*, I replied. When I observed that she was so desperate about me taking advantage of the visa lottery, I agreed to enroll for a couple just for 300 naira, even though I had no wife but a fiancé whom I met about three months before that day.

I registered for both of us and went on my way in annoyance that she wasted my hour for a game of probability. Surprisingly the following year, after my wedding and as we were expecting our first child; I received a call that I won a diversity visa to America, it was like a dream my wife and I were given the immigrant visa for permanent residency status and by His grace I am now a citizen . Hallelujah!

What I am saying is that God can position a man but in actual sense an Angel who will ensure your blessings get to you, I always wish I could see that lady again to bless her for what she did but I couldn't, nevertheless I ascribe the glory to God. It is not in any man's capacity to help me it is God who is working for me. By wisdom approach your Angel can be your wife, husband, neighbor, church member, family member, friends, stranger,   colleague or boss at work and ministers of God.

The Angels in question can also be a group of people, a corporate body such as organization or a community. Government of a country or a nation depending on the magnitude of what God has purposed to do for you in life. The recognition of the simple revelation behind the fact that Angels are on assignment is a sure proof that God will supply you with the right Angel for your next level and you will know that indeed the Lord saves His anointed with the saving strength of his right hand, according to Psalm 20:6. You are blessed in Jesus name.

We are each of us angels with only one wing, and we can only fly by embracing one another.
Luciano de Crescenzo

CHAPTER 4

CHARITY

This book will not be fully beneficial if I fail to acknowledge the importance of charity especially in the Christendom, someone once said to be fruitful is costly. That cost is charity. Then what is charity? It is a system of giving money, food, or help freely to those who are in need. Charity is different from bribe; there are political charity and biblical charity. In the world of politics most charity is a bribe in disguise but biblical charity comes from a pure heart. According to 1 Timothy 1:5, *"Now the end of the commandment is charity out of a pure heart, and of a good conscience, and of faith unfeigned:"*

Approximately at 3a.m I was out early for work which is about two hours' drive from home. I stopped at the gas station to fuel my car, a man walked up to me asking for money to fill his car. I told him I would have helped him but I didn't have enough cash on me. He said I should make use of my credit or debit card. I was surprised at this request but I had a thought within my spirit "what if" this man is an Angel in disguise. I went into my wallet and gave him all the cash I had left and went on my way. The lesson I want to put across is that in our expectation to receive the help of Angels, we should develop an attitude to charity day or night. Hebrew 13:2 says *"Be not forgetful to entertain strangers: for thereby some have entertained angels unawares."*. Most beggars may not be actual beggars we think they are but could be Angels in disguise. That is why I said in the early part of this book that we need God to open the eyes of our understanding to know and discern when the Angel descend in the likeness of man to do us favor. Maybe Abraham's season of barrenness would have lasted a few more years if he had disregarded the company of Angels that passed through his compound. I love the declaration of the Angel *"And He said to Him where is Sarah is your wife? So he said here in the tent"* **And He said "I will certainly return to you according to the time of life, and behold Sarah your wife shall have a son". [Sarah was listening in the tent door which behind him]** Gen. 18:10.

It therefore occurred to me that God promises will come to pass based on your ability to walk in revelation, see things beyond its physical manifestation. Not every delay is orchestrated by our house enemy but because the eyes of our understanding is deem. Our spiritual antenna is not getting the right signal about what we see and hence delay persist. I love the prayer of Apostle Paul for the Ephesians in chapter 1:17-19,

17 That the God of our Lord Jesus Christ, the Father of glory, may give unto you the spirit of wisdom and revelation in the knowledge of him:

18 The eyes of your understanding being enlightened; that ye may know what is the hope of his calling, and what the riches of the glory of his inheritance in the saints,

19 And what is the exceeding greatness of his power to us-ward who believe, according to the working of his mighty power,

This prayer sounds very exclusive to me, being that it informs me of the purpose of opening the eyes of my understanding and shows me what God is capable and able to do for His children in truth. This could be your prayer too. There is power in God's word! Praise God.

In driving home my point, being committed to charity is not a waste of resources. It is said when prayer is delayed, you switch to praise, I say to you also add charity, you will be amazed. A life without charity can end up in shambles. According to Mike Murdock, **"Whatever you make happen for others, will happen for you"**. This statement is synonymous to the law of reciprocal. Whatever you make happen to the house of God happens for you, whatever you make happen to the Ministers of God happens for you, whatever you make happen to your neighbors happens for you. No wonder the Ten Commandments was majorly classified into two broad headings; **"LOVE TO GOD and LOVE TO MAN"**. Mark 12:30-31, one simple way to show the love is charity, then faith, and hope would delivers our

Life is a tapestry: We are the warp; angels the weft; God, the weaver. Only the weaver sees the whole design.

Eileen Elias Freeman 1994

expectations. *And now abideth faith, hope, charity, these three; but the greatest of these is charity.* 1 Corinthian 13:13.

Psalm 107:9 says *"For he satisfieth the longing soul, and filleth the hungry soul with goodness."* As we do so the Lord will satisfy our heart desires and send Angels to us. Amen.

All God's angels comes to us disguised
~ **James Russell Lowel**

AFTERWORD

In conclusion, I will like to say that the greatest assignment of an Angel is the singing ministry and this is not unto man but to God the father, the Son, and the Holy Spirit. [Trinity].

Revelation 4:8 says, *"And the four beasts had each of them six wings about him; and they were full of eyes within: and they rest not day and night, saying,*

Holy, holy, holy
Lord God Almighty,
which was, and is, and is to come;

Revelation 4:9-11 says,

9 And when those beasts give glory and honour and thanks to him that sat on the throne, who liveth for ever and ever,

10 The four and twenty elders fall down before him that sat on the throne, and worship him that liveth for ever and ever, and cast their crowns before the throne, saying,

11 Thou art worthy,
O Lord, to receive glory and honour and power:
for thou hast created all things,
and for thy pleasure they are and were created.
You are worthy, O Lord,

Hallelujah!

This is a revelation of John who saw the Angels in heaven performing their divine assignments. Therefore the Angelic ministry is both relevant to God and humanity. To write about the Angel is not to worship any Angel but to appreciate God for such a wonderful creature to glorify Himself and to make life easy for humanity.

Psalm 8:4-5 says, *"What is man, that thou art mindful of him? and the son of man, that thou visitest him? For thou hast made him a little lower than the angels, and hast crowned him with glory and honour."*

The easiest way God can visit a man is by the Angelic ministration.

Insight is better than eyesight when it comes to seeing an angel.

Eileen Elias
Freeman 1994

Colossians 3:16 says, *"Let the word of Christ dwell in you richly in all wisdom; teaching and admonishing one another in psalms and hymns and spiritual songs, singing with grace in your hearts to the Lord."*

Having said this by Apostle Paul I think in our expectation for Angelic intervention two things will bring them down:

1. **The Word of God with Prayers.**
2. **Hymns and Spiritual Songs.**

These tools are the unbeatable combinations that can easily deliver your long awaiting blessing and as you put them to practice the Lord will release His Angels to minister to you and your testimony will be louder. Amen.

Hymns and Spiritual Songs

Do not let anyone who delight in false humility and the worship of angels disqualify you for the prize. Such a person goes into great detail about what he has seen and his unspiritual mind puffs him up with idle motion.

Colossian 2:18

Hymns and Spiritual Songs

"My Hope is Built on Nothing Less"
by Edward Mote, 1797-1874
1. My hope is built on nothing less
Than Jesus' blood and righteousness;
I dare not trust the sweetest frame,
But wholly lean on Jesus' name.
On Christ, the solid Rock, I stand;
All other ground is sinking sand.
2. When darkness veils His lovely face,
I rest on His unchanging grace;
In every high and stormy gale
My anchor holds within the veil.
On Christ, the solid Rock, I stand;
All other ground is sinking sand.
3. His oath, His covenant, and blood
Support me in the whelming flood;
When every earthly prop gives way,
He then is all my Hope and Stay.
On Christ, the solid Rock, I stand;
All other ground is sinking sand.
4. When He shall come with trumpet sound,
Oh, may I then in Him be found,
Clothed in His righteousness alone,
Faultless to stand before the throne!

On Christ, the solid Rock, I stand;
All other ground is sinking sand.

AMAZING GRACE

Amazing grace! How sweet the sound
That saved a wretch like me!
I once was lost, but now am found;
Was blind, but now I see.

1. 'Twas grace that taught my heart to fear,
And grace my fears relieved;
How precious did that grace appear
The hour I first believed.

2. Through many dangers, toils and snares,
I have already come;
'Tis grace hath brought me safe thus far,
And grace will lead me home.

3. The Lord has promised good to me,
His Word my hope secures;
He will my Shield and Portion be,
As long as life endures.

4. Yea, when this flesh and heart shall fail,
And mortal life shall cease,
I shall possess, within the veil,
A life of joy and peace.

5. The earth shall soon dissolve like snow,
The sun forbear to shine;

But God, who called me here below,
Will be forever mine.
When we've been there ten thousand years,
Bright shining as the sun,
We've no less days to sing God's praise
Than when

Prayer Points

And He will send his angel with loud trumpet call, and they
will gather his elect from the four winds, from one end of the
heaven to the other.
Mathew 24:31.

Prayer Points

Job 22:28, *"You will also declare a thing, and it will be established for you; so light will shine on your ways."*

At the mention of the name of Jesus pray as follow:

1. Thank God for His Angels whom he has made a spirit and His ministers whom he made a flame of fire (Psalm 104:4)

2. Thank God for His love for man (John 3:16)

3. Oh Lord let your Angels surround me and my family day and night (Psalm 121:3-8)

4. Oh Lord send your Angels to open doors of great opportunity for me (Isaiah 45:2-3)

5. Oh Lord send your Angels to me in the likeness of man to help me in life (Genesis 18)

6. Oh Lord let every Goliath that has denied God His glory in my life be struck to death by your Angel (Act 12:23)

7. Oh Lord let your Angel roll away every barrier to my destiny fulfillment In Jesus Name (Mathew 28:2)

8. Every demonic Angel [prince of Persia] that wants to stop my blessing from coming to me fall down and freeze In Jesus Name. (Daniel 10:13)

9. Oh Lord let your Angel complete His divine assignment in my life In Jesus Name (Act 12:10)

10. Oh Lord let your Angel return to me and complete every abandoned project in my life , be it business, marriage, and ministry (Judge 13)

11. Every Angel that has left me I ask that the Lord will bring them back so that my joy shall be full. May be your biological or spiritual parents, husband, wife, uncle, brother, course mate, business partner, children, customers. Church members, etc.

12. **Daniel 6:24 says,** *"My God sent His Angel and shut the lions mouths so that they have not hurt me because I was found innocent before Him"* Oh Lord send your Angel to shut every lions mouths in my father's house. **(Lions are carnivorous animal that feed on flesh. Therefore we are using it figuratively to depict the enemies that can stop our vision.)**

13. 1 Sam 18:1 *"Now when he has finished speaking to Saul, the soul of Jonathan was knit to the soul of David and Jonathan loved him as his own soul."* Oh Lord connect me to a friend that matter in life, people that will show true love and ready to assist me in my finances, marriage, ministry, business and career.

14. Oh Lord let your Angel separate every ungodly friend from my life. (Some friends are evil, some relationship are deadly).

15. Oh Lord let your Angel bring me out of evil relationships and companions.

16. **Nahum 1:13 "For now will I break his yoke from off thee and I will burst thy bond asunder"** Lord send your angel to remove every bondage from my body.

17. **Now Joshua was clothed with filthy garments, and was standing before the Angel. Then He answered to those who stood before him saying "Take away the filthy garments from him And to him He said I have removed your iniquity from you and I will clothe you with rich robe" Zechariah 3:3-4.**

Oh Lord let your angel remove bad identity from my life and clothe me with favor and goodness. In Jesus Name.

Thank God for answering your prayers In Jesus Name.

Do not forget to entertain strangers, for by so doing some have
entertained angels without knowing it.

Hebrew 13:2

OTHER BOOK WRITTEN BY THE AUTHOR

"The Mystery Of The Word And Numbers"

To correspond with the author or for information regarding ministry events or invitations please email him at sijiyokun@gmail.com or call 1-832-576-5233 and 1-832-258-9023

For comments, advise, suggestions and or criticism please be free to contact the author.

This book and other books by the author are available online and at bookstores near you.

God bless you.

QUOTES

Angels have no philosophy but "LOVE" ~ Terry Guillemet.

Praise the LORD, you his angels, you mighty ones who do
his bidding, who obey his word.
Psalm 103:20

The wings of angel are often found on the back of the least
likely people.
Eric Honeycutt.

Pay attention to your dreams – God's angels often speak directly
to our hearts when we asleep.
Eileen Elias Freeman 1994

Angels fly at light speed because they are servants of light
Eileen Elias   Freeman 1994

For the son of man is going to come in his father's glory
with His angels and then He will reward each person according
to what he has done.
Mathew 16:27.

We are each of us angels with only one wing, and we can
only fly by embracing one another.
Luciano de Crescenzo

Life is a tapestry: We are the warp; angels the weft; God, the
weaver. Only the weaver sees the whole design.
Eileen Elias Freeman 1994

Philosophy will clip an angel's wings
~ John Keats

All God's angels comes to us disguised
~ James Russell Lowel

For it is written; "He will command his angels concerning
you to guard you carefully
Luke 4:10

Insight is better than eyesight when it comes to seeing an angel.
Elias Freeman 1994.

I feel that there is an angel inside me whom I am constantly
shocking.
Jean Cocteau.

Angels can illuminate the thought and mind of man by
strengthening of vision.
St Thomas Aquinas.

In Heaven an angel is nobody in particular
~ George Bernard Shaw.

If trouble hearing angels' song with thine ears, Try listening
with the heart.
Terry Guillemets.

Angels can fly because they carry no burdens
~ Eileen Elias Freeman.

In every Heart…. Awaits Your angel.
~ Michael @where Angels Come

Whether we are filled with joy or grief, our angels are close
to us, speaking to our hearts of God's love.
Elias Freeman.

Let us not be justices of peace but, Angels of peace.
Therese de Lisieux.

The magnitude of life is overwhelming. Angels are here to
help us take it peace by peace.
~ Lavender Walters

Angels are spiritual energy
~Alexis Flora Hope, 2007.

Are not all angels ministering spirits sent to serve those who
will inherit salvation?
Hebrew 1:14.

If you can't hear angels try quieting the static of worry.
Terri Guillemets.

God not only sends special angels into our lives, but sometimes He even sends them back again if we forget to take notes the first time .
Eileen Elias Freeman, 1994

Angels will not disintegrate with Logic, but they are more likely to fly for those who believe.
Terry Guillemets.

-Anyone can be an angel~ Author unknown

For if God did not spare angels when they sinned, but sent them into hell, putting them into gloomy dungeons to be held for judgement;
2 Peter 2:4.

-While we are sleeping, angels have conversation with our souls.
Authors unknown

The doors the angels did not open remain closed
Ijiyokun Seun

If men were angels no government will be necessary.
James Madison.

Reputation is what men and women think of us; charac-
ter is what God and angels know of us.
Thomas Paine

Do not let anyone who delight in false humility and the worship of angels disqualify you for the prize. Such a person goes
into great detail about what he has seen and his unspiritual mind
puffs him up with idle motion.
Colossian 2:18.

Friends are kisses blown to us by angel.
Authors unknown

Do not forget to entertain strangers, for by so doing some
have entertained angels without knowing it.
Hebrews 13:2

And He will send his angel with loud trumpet call, and they
will gather his elect from the four winds, from one end of the
heaven to the other.
Mathew 24:31.

Praise the LORD, you his angels, you mighty ones who do his bidding, who obey his word.

Psalm 103:20

NOTES

www.ingramcontent.com/pod-product-compliance
Lightning Source LLC
LaVergne TN
LVHW051156080426
835508LV00021B/2651